simple christmas style

★ style ★

simple christmas style

KARIN HOSSACK

Photographs by Nadia Mackenzie

WATSON-GUPTILL PUBLICATIONS/NEW YORK

Acknowledgements

For the furniture: Verandah, 15B Blenheim Crescent, London W11 2EE, Tel: 0171 792 9289.
For the furniture accessories: Shaker, Tel: 0171 724 7672; Bailey's, The Engine Shed, Ashburton Industrial Estate,
Ross-on-Wye, Herefordshire, Tel: 01989 563015; Woodhams, Tel: 0181 964 9818; Sommerill & Bishop,
100 Portland Road, London W11, Tel: 0171 221 4566; Myriad, 131 Portland Road, London W11, Tel: 0171 229 1709;
Angel at My Table, 14 High Street, Saffron Walden, Essex, Tel: 01799 528777.
For the flooring: Crucial Trading, Tel: 01562 825656; Fired Earth, 01295 812088.
For the fabric: Osborne & Little, Tel: 0181 675 2255; Jane Churchill, Tel: 0171 730 9847.
For the paint: Farrow & Ball, Tel 0171 351 0273. For the flowers: R & R Saggers, Waterloo House, High Street,
Newport, Nr Saffron Walden, Essex CB11 3PG, Tel: 01799 540858.

Published by MQ Publications Ltd.
254–258 Goswell Road, London EC1V 7EB

First published in the United States in 1998
by Watson-Guptill Publications,
a division of BPI Communications, Inc.
1515 Broadway, New York, NY 10036

Series editor: Ljiljana Baird
Editor: Simona Hill
Series designer: Bet Ayer
Photographer: Nadia Mackenzie
Stylist: Emma Folland

Library of Congress Catalog Card Number: 98-60302
ISBN: 0-8230-4802-0

Printed and bound in Italy
1 2 3 4 5 6 7 8 9/06 05 04 03 02 01 00 99 98

contents

F or many of us, Christmas is a special time of year, a time of celebration and goodwill. It is given to entertaining when family and friends draw close. It marks the end of the year and the start of the holiday season. For children, it is magical with the promise of a visit from Santa and a stocking full of exciting gifts. Christmas is also the time of year when we indulge and lavish attention on our homes.

Simple Christmas Style is for those of us who enjoy the festive preparations, who relish the challenge of decorating our homes and making projects, but without it costing us a fortune. The essential spirit of simple style means clearing away the clutter to make space for the things that really matter.

Minimal without being frugal or warm and comfortable ideas that oughly modern. The overall scheme pine boughs, wreaths and swags understated in their elegance. My by different eras of history and the and cultures throughout the world, inspired by the intricate paper-cut-tive paper-cut window decoration bare, *Simple Christmas Style* offers are elegant, appealing and thor- is fresh and unfussy, with many and a wealth of projects which are choices incorporate projects inspired traditions of foreign communities such as the cut-paper shelf edging, ting techniques of Mexico, the narra-inspired by Swiss folk art and the Christmas wheat sheaf, an idea adapted from rural Scandinavia.

Simple Christmas Style features a range of tasteful and innovative yuletide decorations for you to

make. Whether you decide to make floral arrangements to keep the children entertained for an afternoon, or to create a practical Christmas day table-setting, *Simple Christmas Style* has something to offer. My choice of projects is deliberately restrained and restful, no glitzy ornaments or tired old tinsel – these were firmly consigned to the attic. Instead I have designed a range of projects which make effective use of materials to be found

6 ◀

around the house or in the yard. No project requires a trip to a specialty store for unheard of, or extravagant materials, and none requires massive amounts of preparation, assembly time or well-honed craft skills. My projects are all suitable for beginners willing to try their hand at a new skill. Whether your home is a city apartment or a house in the country, each project can be adapted to suit the environment in which it will be displayed and to suit your budget and choice of colors.

I have divided my projects into five chapters with a choice of materials ranging from paper, foil, wire, natural resources, fabric, wood, paint, stencils, or beads. Each chapter focuses on a different aspect of traditional decorations, enabling you to concentrate on creating a complete look for different parts of your home.

Most of us find room to put up a Christmas tree and since it is usually the largest of all the holiday decorations we incorporate into our scheme, it is worth taking the time to make it into a truly beautiful focus of attention. I limited my color and design schemes, so that the items I made would complement each other and not be too obtrusive. Similarly in the chapter *At the Table*, my focus is the red velvet tablecloth. Strong, solid, bold colors immediately attract attention and simple seasonal motifs work well, adding to the Christmas theme to provide an attractive place to serve dinner. While many of my project choices are traditional, such as the Christmas stockings and the felt tree skirt, I have deliberately strayed from the usual festive colors of red, gold and green. I hope too that I have managed to create unusual novelties which are appropriately seasonal. The ribbon and ornament curtain, for example, decorates a corner that may not otherwise receive any decorative attention and like the other projects in the same

chapter can be enjoyed as much from the outside of the house as from within. Similarly, the pine cone gatepost decoration offers an original yet understated seasonal decoration. Whatever your level of ability, or however much time you are left with to prepare for the holiday, *Simple Christmas Style* is sure to inspire your decorating ideas, gifts and home accessories.

This year I decided to make a few changes and abandon all the bright shiny ornaments and thread-bare tinsel in favor of a calmer, more sophisticated approach to Christmas. My budget was set and my challenge defined: to completely redecorate my Christmas tree with materials that can be readily found around the house, recycled from last year, or bought economically from a department store. My projects can be made in an afternoon. They do not require any special skills or training and can involve the help of an eager and excited child. The projects will not take months of planning or involve re-arranging furniture to accommodate the work in progress. Each can be worked on as time and inclination permits without the need for hours of concentration.

With all these ideas in mind, I working with felt, paper and plastic: hanging decorations and plastic for

limited my range of techniques to felt for the tree skirt, paper for the the angel tree lights.

I designed the folded paper traditionally associated with patch-tions can be made as bright and infinite number of variations. In addi-dove – an idea reworked from an did I know that my experiment

pine cones, borrowing a technique work. These intricate paper decora-colorful as you choose and have an tion, I introduced a pierced paper old Victorian reference book. Little would turn into a whole flock! If they

are carefully stored, these decorations will last and look good for years to come.

My greatest innovation was made on a whim: to return my utilitarian Christmas lights to the true spirit of their name. From simple circles and plastic, I made small coverings shaped like fairies to fit over my tree lights. Each is designed to grip the light fitting without creating a fire hazard. The lighting is now more subdued and my strings of angels are safe and sturdy enough to be used outdoors.

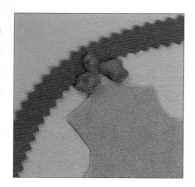

AROUND THE TREE

folded paper pine cones

I first saw a version of these traditional patchwork ornaments on display on a mantel shelf. They were made using printed Christmas muslin cloth. I was struck by the simple yet intricate pattern the folded shapes created and the idea of making "pine cones" to hang from the Christmas tree appealed to me. Wanting to give my cones a contemporary look without taking away from the intricacy of the handcrafting, I chose a selection of beautifully textured handmade Thai and Indian paper. The paper is available in a wide range of colors and is easier to work with than fabric – no frayed edges or awkward folds to press.

Detail of folded patchwork pine cone.

pierced
paper doves

Each year it is so tempting to buy a whole array of glitzy ornaments and beautiful tree decorations. It's so easy to be carried along with the festive preparations and to spend more than your budget may allow.

This year why not spend a few hours in making your own decorations. The satisfaction in creating your own unique projects is immense and the result will be that much more special for you and your family.

These pierced paper doves were inspired by the Victorian era – they look deceptively intricate, but are easy to make. I've kept the doves white, only adding color to the tops of the wings and tails for detail. This allows them to fit easily with any color scheme you may choose for your tree. Once you begin you may find yourself creating a whole flock!

Close up of white pierced paper dove.

paper
gift boxes

At Christmas I'm always tempted to ask for special wrapping, even when the gifts are for my own use, it makes things even more special! Beautifully packaged and presented gifts are always more appealing and add to the festivity of the occasion.

Thinking in this vein, I came to the conclusion that it is worth making the effort to wrap gifts in an interesting way. The wrapping that I've designed could be used for a perfume bottle, or small loose objects that could be trapped between layers of tissue. A simple curl of ribbon on top finishes it off.

This pineapple top box is perfect for packaging home-made truffles or cookies. Just fold over the top and tuck a name tag or greeting card in for the finishing touch.

felt
tree skirt

★

As a child I remember spending many hours sitting and looking at the patterns on the Christmas tree skirt which my mother had made. When the gifts started appearing, the skirt would all but disappear, only to resurface again later on Christmas day.

I made this felt tree skirt in an evening with the help of my son and designed it with seasonal motifs and warm colors in mind. My scheme is deliberately simple, so that the base does not detract attention from the decoration on the tree.

Felt is an easy fabric to work with, and the design does not require any sewing skills. The leaves, stems and berries are simply stuck in place with fabric adhesive.

Detail of stylized holly leaf, pinked stems and "knotted" berries.

angel
tree lights

A child's Christmas school project inspired me to create a disguise for my tree lights. Angels were cut in one piece from a thin cardboard party plate. So simple and so innovative! I adapted the idea, translating non-flammable polypropylene plastic sheeting for the cardboard plate and cut out my shapes by the dozen using pinking shears.

Use the angels as a covering and clip the skirts to standard tree lights for an unusual Christmas decoration.

indow decorations are made for sharing, since they can be admired and enjoyed as much from the outside of the house as from within. As they are intended to be displayed inside the window recess, these decorations provide unobtrusive, uncluttered ornamentation – they will not get broken, stood on, ripped or torn, and can safely be put out of the way of curious little hands. The projects in this chapter offer an economical and practical way to decorate your windows, adding a festive touch to areas that may not otherwise receive decorative treatment.

The decorations I have selected use four different craft techniques – paper craft, ribbon work, stencilling and bead-work. These projects require a little more preparation and planning than those in the preceding chapter and some require special equipment – but the results are worth the effort. Take time when preparing these projects, since inaccuracies cannot be hidden!

Of all my chosen projects, the stencilled frosted window design is probably the most familiar and the easiest to accomplish. The design of reindeers and folk art flowers has a traditional feel and is pleasing and restful to the eye. The repeated motifs also mean that less preparation time is required.

My designs are both traditional and modern, incorporating ideas borrowed and adapted from different cultures. The Swiss paper-cut design can be adapted to suit your window-size using seasonal themes of your own choice. The design can be made as complicated and intricate or as simple and elegant as you choose. Simplified to a smaller scale, this project is appropriate for a child to undertake.

The two remaining projects offer innovative and unusual use of non-traditional materials. The beaded snowflakes and stars are fun to make and will last for years, while the ribbon and ornament curtain can be made fairly quickly with readily available materials to make a practical and attractive window screen.

AT THE WINDOW

s w i s s
p a p e r - c u t

★

Traditional Swiss paper-cut decorations inspired my seasonal sun room window dressing. I've adapted the intricate cutting design found in the original source which was made by master craftspeople to make a simplified and greatly enlarged version. The opaque green waxed paper that I have chosen, lets in natural light so that your living space is not darkened.

The images are true to the spirit of Swiss Christmas traditions: Santa Claus makes his way down the mountain path with his gift laden donkey. Far below a deer looks on as an unsuspecting child enjoys the snow, and a woodcutter gathers his store for the long winter months ahead.

Detail of stylized tree.

Overleaf: Detail of Santa Claus making his way down the mountain path.

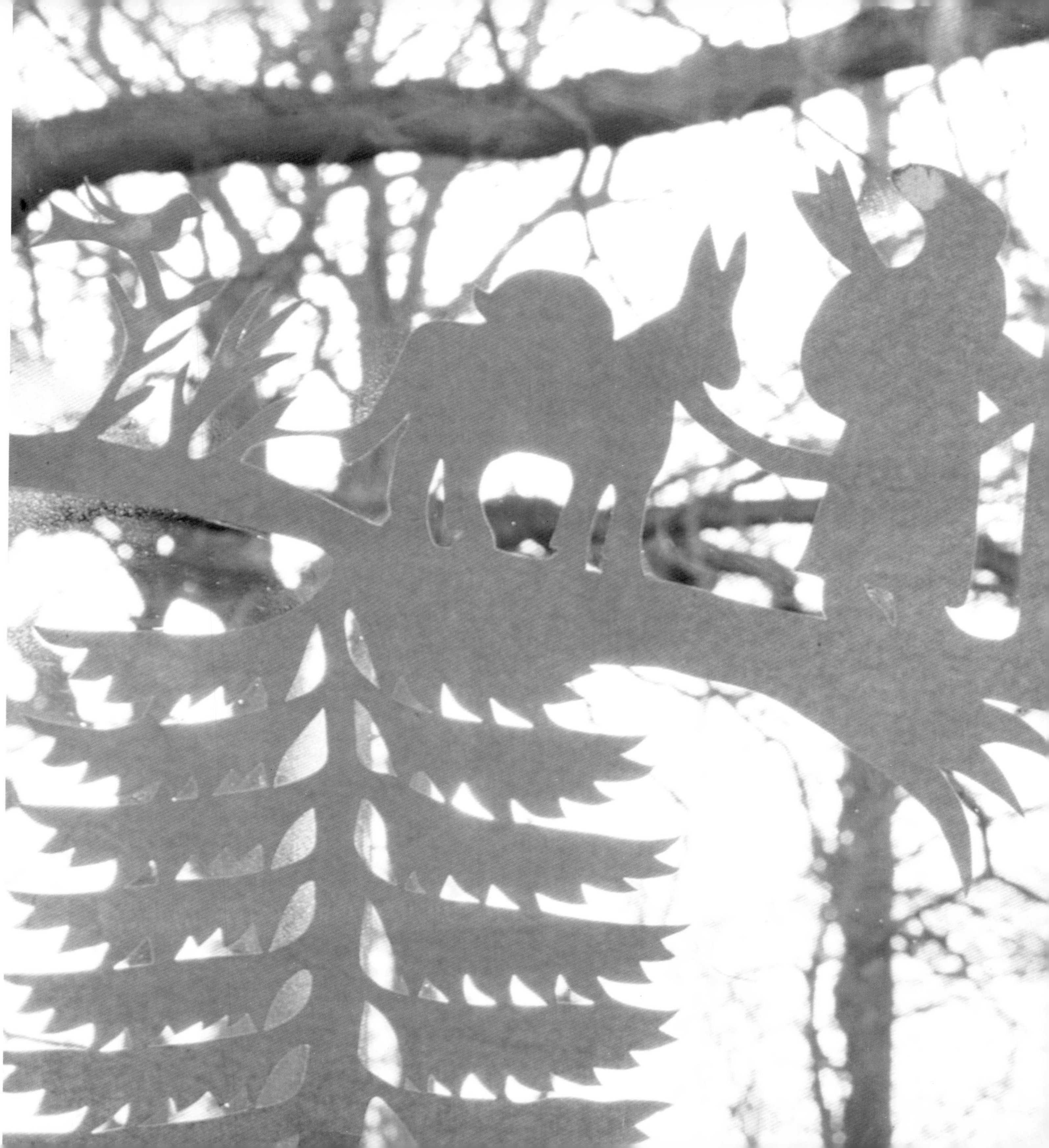

ribbon and ornament curtain

This novel curtain presented me with the opportunity to use up all those ornaments which would not fit on the tree. It effectively adds a sparkle of Christmas color to an otherwise dull corner and adds cheer to an un-decorated window. The ribbon curtain lets in light, decorates your window and retains privacy in your room. The effect is simple, uncluttered and elegant.

The size and shape can be adapted to fit any window and the color-scheme tailored to suit any room. Minimal sewing skills are required – just a good sense of balance and proportion!

Arrangement of ornaments to complement the ribbon and ornament curtain.

frosted window stencil

Frosted windows are an easy way of adding festive holiday charm to your home. Your handiwork will be appreciated from both sides of the glazing. The opaque frosting softens the light but does not darken a room.

In this panelled-window design I've drawn three different images, borrowing ideas from Hungarian and Polish ceramic slipware designs – a proud prancing deer, decorative foliage and flowers. To create the repeat pattern, the stencils are flipped to create mirror images. The stylized folk art floral motifs are reminiscent of delicate snowflakes.

Detail of a decorative foliage design made up of oak leaves, hearts, mistletoe and fringetree.

beaded snowflakes
and stars

Don't let the soldering put you off making these beautiful window decorations. Glass seed beads are attractive to adults and children alike – and these decorations can provide quite an addictive occupation for both. There is a soothing steady rhythm to beading, and making these snowflakes and stars is almost mesmerizing. Fastened together in rows in the windows, these Christmas motifs reflect the light beautifully and provide a glistening, glittering display on a winter's day. They also make an unusual present for anyone who enjoys beads.

Close-up of radiating snowflake center.

accessories

▶ 37

M y choice of projects in this chapter are some of my favorite in the book. Making use of the humblest tools and materials such as paper, scissors, paint, wood, fabric, wheat, winter greenery, pine cones, seed pods and oranges, I have made four beautiful seasonal decorations.

Each of the four projects makes use of a different set of skills from paper-cutting, floral arranging, painting and working with wood to simple sewing and appliqué skills using felt fabric.

Flowers and foliage make your living space into a home, no matter how small or grand that may be. Foliage softens the decor and provides a focus

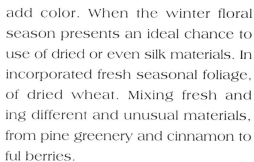

for attention and the opportunity to add color. When the winter floral harvest is sparse, the Christmas season presents an ideal chance to challenge your creativity and make use of dried or even silk materials. In the tradition of Scandinavia, I have incorporated fresh seasonal foliage, abundant in the yard with my sheaf of dried wheat. Mixing fresh and dried allows vast scope for combin- ing different and unusual materials, which are both festive and fragrant, from pine greenery and cinnamon to dried oranges, seed pods and color- ful berries. For those in love with the celebration, and the excitement of

Christmas, I have designed a yuletide angel. Opulent and lavish, painted with an antique gold finish and carrying a fragrant floral garland, this decoration can be refreshed with fragrant materials each year. For the child in all of us, I have designed four beautiful stockings, strong enough to withstand the wear and tear of being tugged and pulled, and filled full with goodies – the only sewing involved is in the embroidered decoration. The stockings are made of durable, machine washable felt and decorated using embroidered details and cut-felt shapes attached with craft glue. Additional decorative details can be added with embroidery and beading.

38 ◀

ACCESSORIES

christmas
wheat sheaf

In rural Scandinavia, wheat sheaves with greenery at their center are traditionally displayed outdoors in front of homes to tempt and sustain birds through the long winter. They symbolize the promise of a bountiful spring. The tradition is founded on the pagan belief that evergreen foliage is the symbol of life renewing itself in the bleak and barren Winter.

Fresh seasonal foliage mixed with dried wheat makes a beautiful decoration for the home, on a mantelpiece or as a table centerpiece. I've used holly with vibrant red berries to tempt these fine-feathered straw birds to stay and rest awhile by the warmth of the fire.

▶ 41

Ornamental bird and berries nesting in the crown of holly on the top of the wheat sheaf.

christmas stockings

As a symbol of bounty and giving, a stocking to hang by the fireplace adds the finishing touch to all your Christmas decorations. This is a project that is definitely worth making for it can be personalized with any number of decorative features.

The felt that I chose is flameproof, machine washable, and comes in a wide range of unusual colors. Felt is such an easy fabric to work with no fraying seams that are difficult to deal with. Once you've traced the pattern, you can make these stockings as simple and understated or as bold and decorative as you choose. Hand-embroidered snowflakes, punched holes, and felt leaves and berries applied using craft glue are just a few of the simple techniques you can use.

Embroidered star detail on the corner of the stocking.

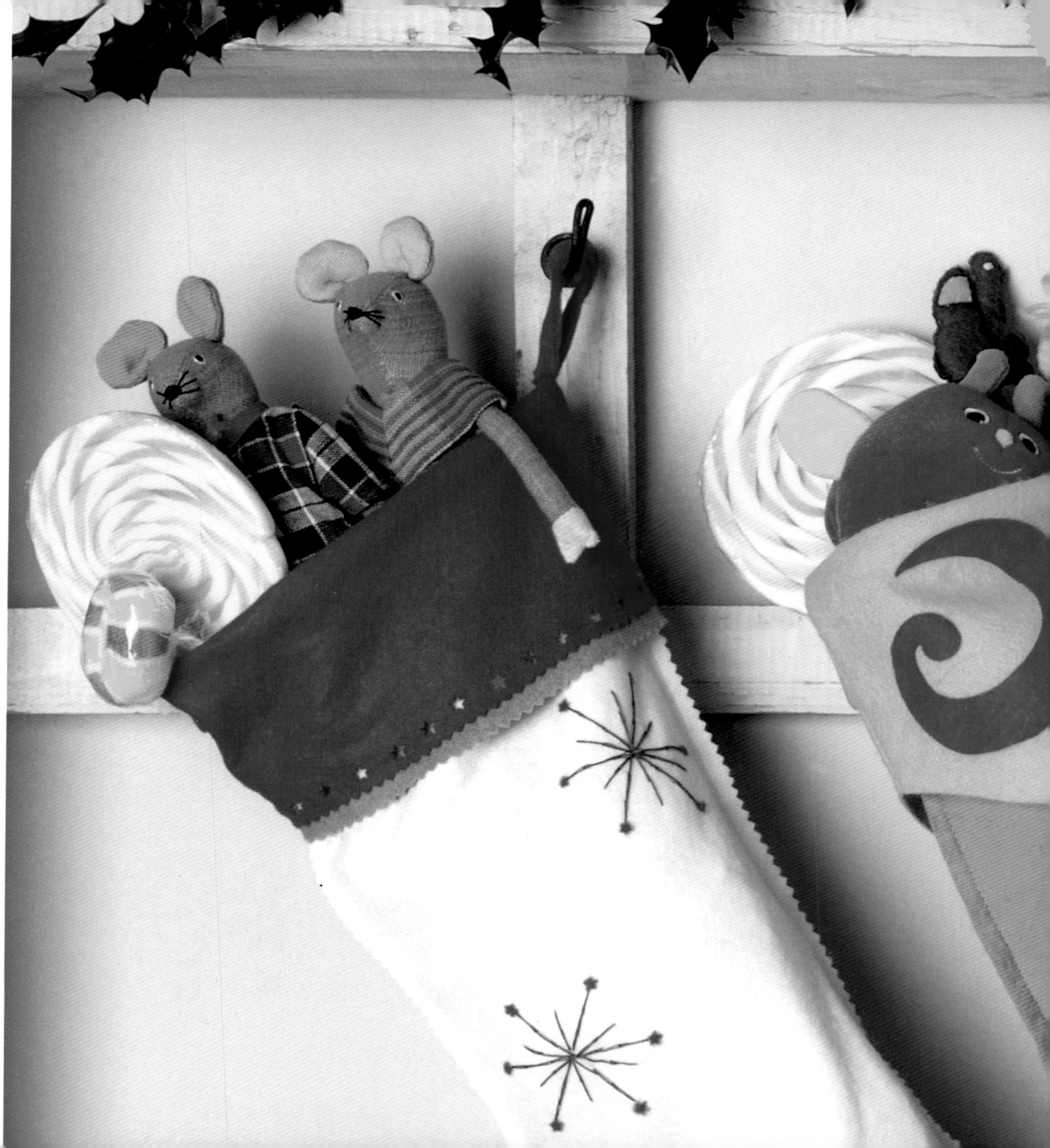

herald angels
swag

I love the image of angels proclaiming the Christmas message of Christ's birth with joyful song. I imagine them hovering over the fireplace, on the tree or taking flight along the banisters loudly rejoicing in the holiday festivities.

Attach these trumpeting angels to a pine swag made of cinnamon sticks, citrus fruits, dried seed pods, nuts, berries and pomanders to create a welcoming seasonal fragrance. Color the angels gold, appropriate for the season of goodwill.

Detail of pine swag decorated with fruits, bundles of cinnamon sticks, nuts, dried seed pods and flowers.

cut-paper
shelf edging

We can probably all recall the fun of cutting paper snowflakes or crêpe paper chains to make Christmas decorations as small children. This edging, though more sophisticated in appearance is made using the same principle – lengths of paper folded over accordion style with shapes cut away from the folds.

This technique has been developed into an art form in Mexico where craftsmen specialize in paper-cutting. Layer upon layer of tissue paper is folded and cut with a hammer and chisel! Their workmanship is displayed across walls in their homes or adorning altars in churches. My design, though not so complicated, is intended to be cut six layers at a time, substituting the hammer and chisel for a craft knife and cutting mat.

The edging can be made as long or short as you choose – simply tape paper lengths together until the required length is achieved.

at the table

At Christmas the dining table is the focus of our attention – more often than we may realize. It is the constant center of our entertaining, and the place where family and friends gather. In recognition of our time spent at the table I wanted to create a sumptuous and elegant setting – one that would be appropriate for the festivities and add to the sense of celebration.

The result is four different projects – a luxurious thick pile embossed velvet tablecloth, a delicate hand-appliquéd organdy tablerunner, exquisite twig reindeer to be used as a table centerpiece and gorgeous beaded flower holders. The velvet tablecloth is suitable for dinner parties and entertainment on a grand scale or simply to dress the table over the Christmas period.

My choice of techniques in this chapter range from the more innovative to the traditional. I decorated my tablecloth with a feast of fruits and flowers, embossing the rayon pile using the heat of an iron. The technique is so simple and effective. In contrast, the tablerunner, is decorated in a random pattern with appliqué motifs of hearts, partridges and pears. For this you will need practiced sewing skills. Traditional appliqué is not difficult, the art is in making the stitches as inconspicuous and as neat as possible. These simple decorations, which highlight the beautiful fabrics are elegant and uncluttered and embody the essence of simple style.

To add an unusual centerpiece to my table, I fashioned reindeers from twigs, cut from an old dogwood tree in the garden. Made on a small scale, these reindeer will fit comfortably on a fully laden Christmas table – that way your handiwork can be admired throughout the course of the dinner instead of moved aside to make room for the dishes.

My final idea was to make a small gift for each of my dinner guests. Everyone loves to receive something handmade, and these beaded flower holders are small enough not to take too long to make and large enough to be appreciated as a thoughtful seasonal gesture. Individualize each one with different beads and add foil-wrapped chocolates or flowers for the final touch.

appliqué tablerunner

This delicate project will appeal to all those who enjoy hand stitching. Using the traditional appliqué method, I applied partridges, pears and hearts to a sheer background. A simple hemming stitch holds each shape in place with additional embroidery stitchery to define the birds' features.

Close-up heart appliqué.

beaded
flower holders

★

Everyone loves to receive a gift, and these beaded flower holders are sure to be admired – the work involved is minimal and the appreciation of the gesture always enthusiastic! Although they look painstakingly intricate, in fact they are quite easy to make. Adjust the size of the bead to one that you are comfortable working with – the rest is addictive!

Fill each pot with a small gift wrapped in colorful tissue or wrap each around a small container filled with fresh seasonal flowers and foliage.

Detail of beads threaded on wire frame.

embossed velvet
tablecloth

While your instincts may tell you never to use a luxury fabric for a tablecloth, this one can be washed in the machine without fear of ruining the pile. More than any other fabric, sumptuous velvet in a rich jewel-like shade is perfect for the celebration of Christmas.

All you need to recreate this embossed tablecloth is a hot iron and a rubber stamp – make your own or choose from the many designs available through special stamp suppliers. I chose an arrangement of pomegranates, stylized acanthus leaves and lush grapes to represent the festive bounty of the Christmas feast.

▶ 59

Detail of pomegranate motif on the velvet tablecloth.

t w i g
r e i n d e e r

★

These serene and elegant reindeer are quickly con-
structed from the branches of a dogwood tree and
simple garden twine. No two will ever be alike and the
challenge is in effectively manipulating the branches
into the correct shape. The skills required are simple – a
whole herd will have appeared before you know it and
the dogwood tree in the yard will be bereft of branches!

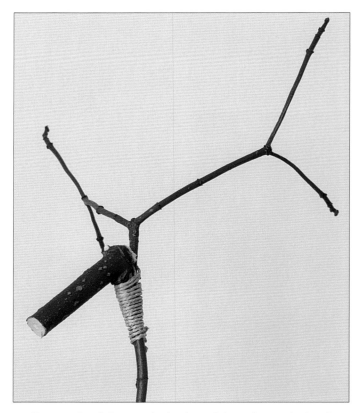

Close-up detail showing the binding of the antlers to the head.

Since pagan times, wreaths and garlands of seasonal flowers and foliage have been used to decorate the home and more specifically the front door. In ancient times, evergreens were revered for their ability to endure the winter and to remain green when all outside was barren and grey. For a primitive population dependent on the land for survival, these trees represented life. Over time, evergreen foliage became associated with bringing luck and a wreath hanging on the door was guaranteed to ward off evil spirits, as well as being a symbol of welcome.

With so many ways of constructing wreaths using moss and twigs as a base and with such a

wealth of materials available to us, your choice of wreath decoration can be as varied and individual as your imagination allows. For this final chapter, I have designed four different floral decorations, each inspired by the traditional wreath, but each thoroughly modern in interpretation. My foil-covered chocolate wreath will appeal to those with a sweet tooth – cute enough to be suitable for a child, and sophisticated enough to hang on any inside door. Tailor your choice of chocolate candies to suit the recipient of the gift.

As with all wreaths, the base material will determine the lifespan of your decoration. Since the chocolate wreath will probably have a short lifespan I chose to use a thick corrugated cardboard base which can be disposed of as soon as the chocolates have been removed!

Similarly the pine cone gatepost decoration will last only as long as the weather allows – so my materials are economical and most can be found in the yard. The acorn and vine wreath is elegantly sparse but made beautiful with a touch of gold to the leaves. It is best displayed hung against a plain wooden door.

No Christmas decor is complete without the presence of the traditional bough of mistletoe in the house. My mistletoe kissing bough is deliberately lavish and beautifully delicate, hovering gracefully from the ceiling. The fine twisted and curled wire frame will last for years.

BY THE DOOR

chocolate wreath

A modern reworking of the traditional pine wreath shows how old ideas can be adapted and updated. A Christmas decoration that can be eaten makes an ideal gift and an enjoyable project for those with a sweet tooth. The pine wreath to which the chocolates are attached is made from corrugated cardboard with the pine branches stuck in place using a glue gun!

I've chosen a variety of colorful insects, birds and fruit to adorn the wreath – oversize lady-bugs, smiling bumble bees, bright butterflies and liqueur-filled orchard fruits – all sure to attract takers from far and wide.

Detail of foil-covered chocolates and candies used to decorate the pine wreath.

BY THE DOOR

acorn and vine wreath

The most mundane of jobs provided the inspiration for this rustic acorn wreath. As I cleared and pruned the trees and bushes in my yard in the early winter months and cut back a straggling honeysuckle, my attention turned to recycling the cuttings and rakings which would otherwise be cast on the compost heap.

   I entwined and wrapped the longest cuttings from the honeysuckle branches, forcing them into an oval shape while the vines were full of sap and still pliable. To my basic structure I added soft brown acorns wired together and undulating oak leaves painted in gold for a rich finish.

Detail of painted gold oak leaves and acorns wired to the vine oval-shaped frame.

mistletoe kissing bough

This beautiful mistletoe kissing bough will catch every-one's attention hanging close to the front door, in a hallway or high-ceiling room. Sprigs of mistletoe are entwined with delicate curling, twisted wires and gently ringing bells. Two wire circles are held together with simply-constructed springs and the whole is sus-pended from the ceiling with a huge wire bow – the perfect shelter for a Christmas kiss.

This design can easily be adapted to fit your ceiling height. Once Christmas is over, alterations can be made by adding fragrant fresh foliage or dried flowers.

Detail of spring-like suspending wires.

Detail of the bow at the top of the bough.

pine cone gatepost decoration

I have often stopped to admire stonework or cement pine cone-shaped ornaments adorning an entrance or humble gatepost. I challenged myself to recreate a similar shape suitable for an external Christmas decoration – one that would withstand the winter elements and at the same time welcome my guests.

My materials are all standard florist's equipment. The pine cones were collected throughout the year on forages in the woods and the countryside.

Close-up of pine cones and wooden berries glued together to make up the gatepost decoration.

putting it together

C hristmas can be expensive, so this year why not plan your decorations to incorporate as many free natural materials as you can find. A walk through the woods or yard should yield pocketfuls of fallen acorns, pine cones, twigs, seed pods, leaves and flower-heads which can be dried or used fresh if picked specially for the project. Plan your walks and outings with care and your harvest will produce special Christmas decorations. Similarly, while working in the garden, choose vines and stems which can be manipulated into wreaths and garlands and bind them into shape as you find them while they are still pliable.

While luck and good planning will form the basis of many floral decorations and table arrangements, most projects have been designed with economy in mind. My

Christmas tree decorations were made using paper over a plastic base and can be as decorative or as plain as you choose. Choose unusual textured papers for a truly stunning effect and store the decorations carefully so that they last for many seasons. With cheap base materials, it is easy to justify spending a little extra on decorative materials which will be seen – pretty ornaments to hang on the ribbon curtain, beautiful beads for the flower holders and unusual chocolates for the chocolate wreath.

Very few of my projects require special materials, the herald angel swag requires the use of a jigsaw, the angle tree lights are made from polypropylene plastic and the base of the snowflakes and stars are soldered together with a blow torch or soldering iron. Otherwise all the other projects in this chapter can be made with equipment found in most domestic sewing baskets and tool kits.

Assemble your tools and materials before beginning to ensure your check list is complete. Careful preparation and planning will always give better results that you can be quite proud of!

PUTTING IT TOGETHER

folded paper pine cones

★

These folded patchwork-style decorations are simple to make using a variety of pretty papers, polystyrene eggs, craft pins and thread.

MATERIALS

◆ *A selection of 3in/7.5cm polystyrene eggs*
◆ *Light-weight handmade papers in a variety of colors – two colors per egg*
◆ *Sequin and bead craft pins*
◆ *Metallic glass bead-head craft pins*
◆ *Lamé embroidery thread*
◆ *Straight edge or ruler*
◆ *Paper scissors*

1 On each of two sheets of contrasting color paper, measure and mark 1¾in/4.5cm wide strips down the length of each sheet. Carefully cut each strip.

2 To make the folded triangle, on one strip, fold the corner of a short end in towards the long side so that straight edges are aligned. Cut the excess strip away from the folded triangle. Make 26 from color A and 24 from color B.

3 Fold each triangle in half.

4 Cut one 1in/2.5cm square of color A. Cover the narrow end of the egg with the square and mold to fit. Pin the corners.

5 Place four triangles of color B over the paper square so that the triangle tips meet at the tip of the egg. Pin each triangle in place on the two narrow points using craft pins. Insert the pins at an angle.

6 Position four triangles of color A ¼in/0.75cm below row 1 and pin in place, so that the tip is staggered between the tops of the previous row.

7 Continue to alternate the colored rows, working around the form and keeping the triangles evenly spaced so that no gaps or pin heads show.

8 When you reach the end, carefully overlap the last four triangles. Cover all of the cut edges with a small square cut from the same color paper. Pin temporarily in place.

9 Make a lamé thread bow. Place on the end of the egg and pin through all the layers with a craft pin.

p i e r c e d   p a p e r   d o v e s

Recreate a timeless classic decoration for your tree with these unusual pierced paper doves, drawn from a Victorian reference.

MATERIALS
- *Two or three sheets of decorated or textured handmade paper*
- *Choice of colors of metallic finish giftwrap paper*
- *Lamé embroidery thread*
- *Scissors, pencil and ruler*
- *Folded towel or blanket*
- *Glue stick*
- *Medium-weight craft cardboard for templates*
- *Large embroidery needle*

1 To make templates, enlarge the patterns provided on page 109 to the desired size. Stick the copy onto cardboard and cut out.

2 On the wrong side of the decorated paper, draw around the body A, wing span B and wing details D templates. Use the metallic paper for the scalloped wing edges C and for the tail E.

3 Cut two of each shape except for the wing span which requires one.

4 Place the dove pieces right side down on a folded towel. Using the embroidery needle and following the pattern on the templates, punch holes through the paper. This step can be worked using two or three pieces of paper together at a time.

5 Glue the curved edge only of wing D to the wing span B using the picture below as a guide. Glue the scalloped wing C to the underside of the wing span B. When dry use your finger to curl out the scalloped edges on the glued pieces.

6 Glue each metallic tail E to a decorated paper tail E. Glue each tail to the underside of each body. Right sides together, fold the wing span B in half across the tab. Glue half of the tab to the underside of the body, just behind the neck bend.

7 Glue on the other side of the body. Bend the wing span B into position.

8 Using a 8in/20cm length of lamé thread, make a stitch through the edge of the body where the wings have been glued. Make a loop and tie with a knot.

► 79

paper gift boxes

★

Make use of beautiful handmade or textured papers to wrap small or unusually shaped gifts in style.

MATERIALS
- ◆ *Heavy-weight paper in your choice of colors*
- ◆ *Double-sided transparent tape, scissors*
- ◆ *Paper punch*
- ◆ *Ribbon or string*
- ◆ *Glue stick*

1 Enlarge the patterns provided and cut out. To make large boxes, enlarge the patterns in sections and stick the pieces together, overlapping and aligning lines as

necessary. If you intend to make many boxes use cardboard for the template.

2 Choose your paper for the box. On the wrong side, draw around the template. Mark all fold lines. Cut out the outline.

3 For the pineapple box, crease all fold lines. Fold in the sides and secure the side tab on the inside of the box with double-sided tape. Push in the bottom tab and secure as before.

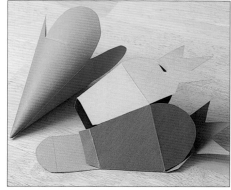

4 Fill the box as desired. Interlink the pineapple top and bend the tab up into a standing position.

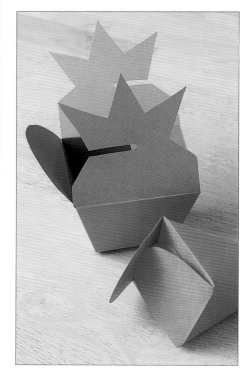

5 For the cone box, crease all fold lines.

6 Find the center of the long edge for the tip, then overlap the edges of the shape tightly to form a cone. Stick the side edge in place.

7 Hold the cone with the point facing down. Fold each flap flat across the top. Secure the last flap with tape. Make a hole near the tip of the cone and thread ribbon or string through it.

felt tree skirt

Wrap unsightly metal stands or practical containers with this felt tree skirt. Felt is easy to work with and the motifs are simply glued in place.

MATERIALS

◆ 1¼yd/1.2cm square of felt in main color
◆ ½yd/0.5m each of contrasting colors for holly leaves and stems
◆ ¾in/2cm-wide strips of red felt for berries
◆ Craft glue
◆ Pinboard pin
◆ Scissors and tape measure
◆ Pinking shears
◆ Tracing paper and pencil
◆ Medium-weight cardboard
◆ Length of string or twine

1 To make the felt circle, fold the main color in half. Find the center of the folded edge and mark this point with a pinboard pin. Tie one end of the string around the pin. Measure 25½in/65cm along the length of string and cut. Tie the free end to a pencil. Working on a flat surface, hold the pin in place and at the same time hold the pencil so that the string stays taut and even.

Draw an arc from one folded edge around to the other side.

2 Measure 4in/10cm from the pin and in the same way draw a small circle.

3 Cut out both circles using pinking shears. Using scissors, cut across one side of the folded edge, from the center, so that the skirt can be opened.

4 From the patterns provided make templates for the holly leaves. Trace the shapes. Stick the tracing paper on cardboard and cut out. On your choice of felt color, draw around each template. Cut nine small, nine medium and 18 large leaves.

5 For the stems, cut ¾in/2cm wide strips each 23¾in/60cm long using pinking shears.

6 For the berries, cut six strips of felt ¼ x 23¾in/0.75 x 60cm. Tie each length into a chain of knots. Cut each knot from the chain. Make 81.

7 Open out the tree skirt. Arrange the stems 31in/80cm apart at the outside edge. Bend each stem into a wavy line, with tight waves at the skirt center and larger waves at the outside edge. Make two curves in one direction and one in the other. When you are happy with the arrangement lightly glue the stems in place.

8 On each stem place one small, medium and large holly leaf so that each fits inside the curves of the stem. Begin with the smallest leaves at the center of the skirt, and the large leaves at the outside edge. Lightly glue each leaf in place.

9 Glue one berry to the top of each small leaf, two berries for each medium leaf and three berries for each large leaf.

angel tree lights

Don't let the unusual material put you off making these innovative tree light coverings. They are easy to make and the materials are readily available from good craft stores.

MATERIALS

- ◆ *A sheet of white polypropylene plastic*
- ◆ *Template plastic or medium-weight cardboard*
- ◆ *Scissors*
- ◆ *Pencil*
- ◆ *Tracing paper*
- ◆ *Pinking shears*
- ◆ *½in/1cm leather hole punch*
- ◆ *Small piece of plywood*
- ◆ *Hammer*
- ◆ *Paper punch*
- ◆ *String of standard tree lights*

1 To make a template, photocopy the pattern provided. Glue the copy to cardboard and cut out. Punch the holes marked on the pattern using a paper punch.

2 Onto white polypropylene plastic draw around the template. Mark the holes and cutting lines.

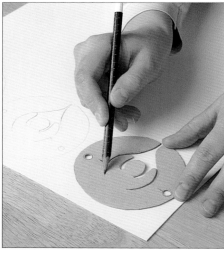

3 Cut out each shape using pinking shears. Cut the head and arms with scissors.

4 With the piece of plywood for a surface, use the leather punch and a hammer to punch the marked holes.

5 Wrap the wings around so that they overlap and slot together.

6 Align the holes in the wings and stick onto the tree lights so that they grip the rubber base of the light fittings.

swiss paper-cut

★

This traditional Swiss paper-cut can be adapted to tell your own version of the Christmas story to fit any window.

MATERIALS

◆ *Heavy-duty green waxed paper –*
sufficient to cover the window surface
◆ *Tracing paper*
◆ *Spray mount, glue stick*
◆ *Scissors*
◆ *Craft knife*
◆ *Cutting mat*

1 Enlarge the pattern provided to the size of the window. Use the grid on the pattern as a guide and enlarge the pattern in sections.

2 Arrange the photocopies in the correct order, overlapping the edges that appear twice. With a glue stick, stick the copies together to form a complete full-size template.

3 Working in sections, place sheets of tracing paper over the design and stick together. Trace the design lines onto tracing paper using a bold line that can be seen through the back of the tracing paper. Redraw the lines where necessary.

4 Use spray mount to stick the tracing paper, drawn side down onto the green waxed paper.

5 Cut out the design. When cutting sections that need joining leave a small overlap on both edges.

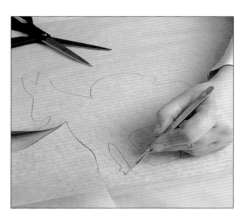

6 Peel off the tracing paper from the back of the paper-cut pieces. Temporarily tape to the window to check the fit.

7 Working in sections, take down one piece at a time and spray the back with spray mount. Remount it onto a clean, dry window in the correct position, overlapping edges as necessary. When the design is in position and the spray mount is dry, use a craft knife to trim back any overlapped edges. Neaten up all edges.

ribbon and ornament curtain

This innovative ribbon curtain makes an unusual screen using non-traditional materials

MATERIALS
- ½in/1.5cm diameter dowel to fit the width of the window
- Two screw eyes
- Two screw hooks
- A variety of widths of grosgrain ribbon in assorted colors
- Sewing thread to match ribbon colors
- Sewing kit
- Dressmaker's hook and eyes – one for each ribbon used
- Saw
- Drill
- Assorted Christmas ornaments – one for each ribbon
- Paint to match shade of ribbons
- Paint brush

1 Measure the length and width of your window.

2 Cut a length of dowel to fit the width of the window plus 1in/2.5cm on each side.

3 Drill holes into the ends of the dowel and screw in screw eyes.

4 Measure and mark the dowel position on the window frame. Drill holes in alignment with the screw eyes and screw the hooks in place in the window frame.

5 Paint the ends of the dowel to match the main color of the ribbons. Allow to dry.

6 Arrange the ribbon lengths side by side on a flat surface. You will need sufficient space to make up the same width as the width of the dowel. Number the ribbon lengths and make a chart detailing the order.

7 The middle ribbon hangs 12in/30cm above the window ledge. To gauge the length of this ribbon, measure the height

of the window, then deduct 12in/30cm. The shortest ribbons hang at each side of the window frame and are half the length of the middle ribbon. Mark the lengths on your chart. The remaining ribbons taper from the middle to the sides. Work out suitable lengths for each and write them on your chart.

8 Add 2in/5cm to each length for seams. Drape the ribbons over the dowel and pin in place to check the fit. When you are happy with the arrangement, remove the dowel.

9 Stick small pieces of masking tape to the top of each ribbon, numbering them in order. Remove the ribbons and stitch each seam in place.

10 Make a 2in/5cm loop in the top of a piece of ribbon and using a matching thread color sew it down, Make sure that the fold is straight, if it is crooked the ribbon will hang incorrectly. Sew all the ribbons in the same way.

11 To make the bottom edges, fold both corners to the back, to form a point. Sew the turned in edges together working from the point to the upper edge.

12 Sew a dressmaker's hook close to the tip of each ribbon at the back.

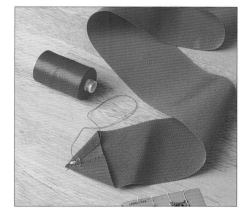

13 Slide all ribbons onto the dowel keeping the correct numerical sequence. Hang on window hooks.

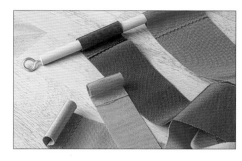

14 Hang a selection of Christmas ornaments onto the hooks at the back of the ribbons.

frosted window stencil

★

Making accurate stencils for the window motifs takes practice, but the effect is worth the effort.

MATERIALS

- ◆ *Glass etch spray can (Krylon)*
- ◆ *Spray mount*
- ◆ *Craft knife*
- ◆ *Cutting mat*

1 Photocopy the three designs, enlarging each to fit your window. You will need four flower and leaf designs and eight copies of the reindeer.

2 Use the photocopies as stencils and cut out each using a *craft knife* on a cutting mat. If you cut any lines in error tape the piece together and continue cutting.

3 Clean the window panes thoroughly and allow to dry.

4 Place the stencils right side down on a sheet of newspaper. Spray lightly with spray mount and apply all the stencils in the desired order to the window panes.

5 Follow the manufacturer's instructions, apply glass etch spray over the window surface. A soft even coat applied twice works best.

6 Allow to dry, then peel away the stencils.

7 To remove the etch spray, scrape away with a single-edged razor or blade.

beaded snowflakes and stars

Tiny glass seed beads in a myriad of colors make an unusual ornamental curtain when wired together.

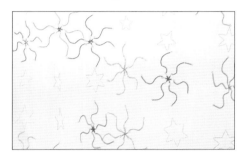

MATERIALS

◆ *1 lb/0.5kg of 0.9mm galvanized steel wire*
◆ *Soldering iron or mini blow torch*
◆ *Solder and flux*
◆ *⅛in/4mm seed beads in assorted colors*
◆ *⅛in/5mm cut glass beads*
◆ *Round-nose pliers and wire snippers*
◆ *Aluminum surface*
◆ *Steel wool*

1 Cut three lengths of 0.9mm wire, each 12in/30cm long, for each snowflake.

2 Clean the film of grease from the center-section of each wire using steel wool.

3 Place three wires on an old aluminum surface. Cross the wires over each other at the center to make a snowflake. The

aluminum surface will not conduct heat and the solder will not stick to it.

4 Solder the wires together at the center using a soldering iron.

5 Heat the wires, then apply a small amount of flux to the center point using a toothpick.

6 Bring the flame back to the center of the wires and touch it with the end of a roll of solder. Keep the heat on the solder until all the wires are bound together. Allow to cool.

7 Slide three seed beads and one cut glass bead onto a wire. Grasp the wire with pliers and bend the end at an angle to stop the beads from falling off as you work around the snowflake.

8 Grasp the wire just above the cut glass bead with a round-nose plier and form a loop in each spoke.

9 Add contrasting color seed beads to each spoke. When you are 1in/2.5cm from the end, grasp the end of the wire with round-nose pliers as before and form a loop on the end of each spoke for a decorative finish.

10 Bend the snowflake just above the loop near the center into a curve. Halfway up the length, bend it back in the opposite direction. Bend all six spokes keeping the shape as even as possible.

christmas wheat sheaf

★

Wear gardening gloves to protect your hands when making this unusual floral decoration.

MATERIALS

- ◆ *Approximately 300 stems of wheat*
- ◆ *8–10 stems of holly with berries*
- ◆ *Florists' wire*
- ◆ *Small decorative birds*
- ◆ *Scissors*
- ◆ *Pliers*
- ◆ *Garden gloves*
- ◆ *Ribbon to trim*

1 Trim each holly stem to 7in/18cm long. Trim any leaves from the base of the stems. Make a tightly formed conical shape, then wire the stems together using florists' wire.

2 Holding the holly in one hand, begin applying wheat in small bunches of three or four stems at a time. Work your way around the holly, holding the wheat stems at an angle. Hold the wheat in place with wire as you work. Continue using the stems until a thick sheaf is formed. Twist wire around the middle of the stems.

3 Trim the bottom of the stems even. Place the sheaf on a table top and arrange the stems at an angle. With scissors flat to the table surface, trim the stems from the bottom to achieve the desired height. Work from the middle out.

4 Attach 8in/20cm lengths of florists' wire to the decorative birds. Place each bird in the holly by pushing the wires securely through the holly into the sheaf.

5 Tie the middle of the sheaf with a ribbon to finish.

christmas stockings

★

Kids will love these big, bold felt Christmas stockings – especially when they're packed full of Santa's surprises!

MATERIALS
- ◆ 20 x 36in/50 x 100cm main color felt for stocking
- ◆ 20 x 8in/50 x 20cm contrast color felt for cuff
- ◆ 12in/30cm square contrast color felt for the cuff decoration
- ◆ Sewing kit
- ◆ Craft glue
- ◆ Scissors
- ◆ Templates
- ◆ Hand and machine embroidery thread to match all three colors of felt

1 Enlarge the patterns provided on pages 108–109 on a photocopier to measure 17½in/45cm from the top to the bottom of the heel.

2 Cut out the photocopies. Draw around the stocking and the cuff on the correct color of felt. Cut two of each.

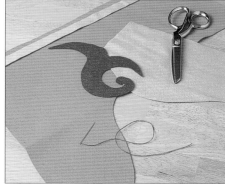

3 From scraps of felt cuff, cut a strip ⅓ x 8in/1 x 20cm. Use this to make the hanging loop.

4 Embroider the six-point stars in a random pattern on the front and back of the stocking using three strands of contrasting color embroidery thread.

5 With right sides together stitch the top of each cuff to the top of each stocking.

6 Sew the cuff side seams together pressing the selvage in the same direction on both sides.

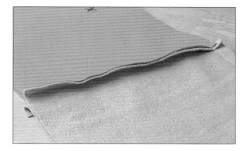

7 Stitch the two halves of the stocking together using a ¼in/0.75cm seam.

8 Fold the cuff down. Embroider a six-pointed star on the cuff or stick on the decoration with craft glue.

9 Fold the hanging loop in half lengthwise. Sew through both layers, from end to end using matching thread. Fold the loop in half and baste the two ends together. Sew in place in inside back of cuff.

▶ 89

herald angels swag

★

Use seasonal foilage and dried fruits in this scented swag.

MATERIALS

◆ ¼in/0.6cm thick medium density fiberboard (MDF) 20 x 32in/50 x 80cm
◆ Jigsaw with medium blade
◆ Gold spray paint
◆ Glue stick
◆ Scissors
◆ Two D rings
◆ Screwdriver
◆ Two ½in/1.5cm slotted brass screws
◆ Garden twine
◆ Masking tape
◆ Fine florists' wire – 22 gauge
◆ Fine grade sandpaper
◆ Drill
◆ Two picture hooks and nails
◆ Sprigs of pine boughs, cinnamon sticks, twine, dried flower heads, dried seed pods, dried orange segments, pine cones, acorns, walnuts

1 Make a template of the angel from the pattern provided. Enlarge the pattern on a photocopier to measure 19in/49cm from the tip of his toe to the end of his trumpet. Draw two on the fiberboard.

3 Sand all the edges smooth with fine grade sandpaper.

4 Spray paint the angels with gold, including all the edges. Allow to dry.

6 To make the swag, cut a length of gardening twine the required length adding to your measurement enough to tie loops at each end. Tie a long loop at one end and secure the loop to a work surface with a piece of masking tape.

7 Cut pine branches into twigs 6in /15cm long. Cut a quantity to begin, then cut more twigs as you need them.

8 Beginning at the secured loop, use wire to tie on the first twig. Hold the next branch in place and wrap the wire around the end of the branch and the twine three times. Wrap the wire back up the branch. Wiring up and down the branch stops the materials from sliding. Add the next twig in the same way. Continue adding pine greenery until the desired length is reached. Tie a long loop in the end.

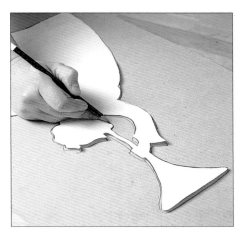

2 Cut out two angels. Drill holes in the space between the forearm and chin, large enough to fit the jigsaw blade, then continue cutting.

5 Find the point of balance near the top of the wings by holding an angel between your thumb and forefinger. Mark the point of balance and screw a D ring in place with a small brass screw. Take care not to puncture the front of the angel.

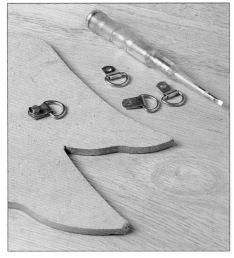

9 Fill in any bare areas by tying in sprigs of pine with short lengths of wire.

10 Decorate the garland by wiring into position dried fruit, flowers and nuts and foliage of your choice.

11 Hang the pine swag in positionl, then add the angels to each side.

cut-paper shelf edging

★

The traditional skills of Mexican craftsmen have been adapted to make this ornate shelf edging.

MATERIALS

◆ *Roll of colored waxed paper*
◆ *Roll of white or transparent waxed paper*
◆ *Cutting mat, craft knife and blades*
◆ *Paper clips and black marker*
◆ *Pinking shears*

1 Measure the width of your shelf and determine the drop of the edging. Enlarge the template to fit an even number of times into the shelf width. Define the cut out shapes with a black marker. For a long length, make several copies.

2 Cut the required length of colored and white waxed paper. Stick the lengths together. Fold each length accordion-style to the same width as the template.

3 Slide the template into the folded colored paper, sandwiching it between the third and fourth fold. Make sure that you can see the definition of the design lines through the top layer. If you have more than six layers, simply unfold the remaining layers of paper from the bottom of the stack and leave them to one side.

4 Secure all four corners of the stack with paper clips to prevent the folds from slipping.

5 Place the stack on the cutting mat and carefully cut out the design. With a new, sharp blade you should be able to cut through six layers of paper and the template at the same time. Use a new template for each stack of six sheets.

6 Cut the scalloped edge with pinking shears. Remove the paper clips.

7 Slide a template inside the white waxed paper as before. Draw the scalloped edge with a pencil. Remove the template and cut on the line using pinking shears. Remove the paper clips.

8 Unfold both accordions. Place the white paper-cut behind the colored paper, all edges aligned. Slide the white paper down so that it sits 1in/2.5cm below the colored paper. Stick the layers together. Fold the top edge over so that it creates a shelf lining, or cut it off and stick both layers of paper-cut to the edge of the shelf.

appliqué tablerunner

★

Traditional appliqué skills are needed for this beautiful white organdy tablerunner.

MATERIALS

- ◆ ½yd/0.5m white linen
- ◆ 43 x 25in/110 x 64cm white cotton organdy
- ◆ Sewing kit
- ◆ Scissors
- ◆ Four cloth-covered or shell buttons
- ◆ Iron
- ◆ Tracing paper, pencil and glue stick
- ◆ Medium-weight cardboard

1 To make templates, trace the patterns provided on page 111. Stick the tracings to the cardboard and cut out.

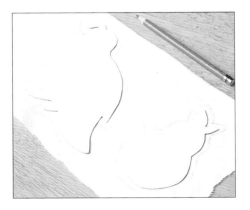

2 Draw around each template onto the linen adding a ¼in/0.75cm seam all around. Cut out six birds, six pears, two leaves and two hearts, cutting just inside the pencil line.

3 Turn in the ¼in/0.75cm seam all around each and baste to secure. Use long stitches and tie the thread on the front. Use colored thread for basting.

4 Press each piece with a hot steam iron.

5 Turn in a ½in/1.5cm seam twice around the raw edge of the organdy. Press and blindhem in place.

6 Arrange the appliqué shapes as desired on the organdie background and pin in place.

7 With white thread, sew each shape in place using small, neat stitches. Remove the pins as you work. Remove all basting stitches.

8 Embroider French knot eyes on each part ridge. Add three running stitch veins to the middle of each leaf and add a detail line to the wing of each partridge.

▶ 93

9 To erase the pin markings, hand wash the runner in cold water using a gentle detergent. Iron when dry with a hot steam iron.

10 Sew one button to each corner.

beaded flower holders

Beadwork appears delicate and intricate but is actually simple to accomplish. Once the strands are wired together, these containers are very sturdy.

MATERIALS

◆ ⅛in/4mm seed beads in two colors (A and B)
◆ ¼in/6mm pressed glass beads – 14 for each pot (C)
◆ Round-nose pliers
◆ Flat-nose pliers
◆ Wire snippers
◆ 0.6mm silver-plated wire
◆ Glass container to insert in holder
◆ Fresh flowers
◆ Foliage
◆ Florist's oasis block

1 For each beaded pot, cut one length of wire 7in/18cm long.

2 With round nose pliers, form a ⅛in/2mm closed loop in one end. This is the base wire for the holder.

3 Cut 14 lengths of wire 3½in/9cm long.

4 Form a ⅛in/2mm closed loop in one end of each, these are the eye pins.

5 Thread four seed beads from B on the base wire.

6 Thread on an eye pin, then four more beads and an eye pin.

7 Thread on 56 beads in total finishing with an eye pin.

8 Pick up the open end of the wire in the round-nose pliers.

9 Thread on the loop at the opposite end and the loop of the last eye pin. Twist the wire to close the loop.

10 Arrange the beadwork on a flat work surface. Stand one eye pin up and thread the following beads on: 1 x B, 1 x A, 1 x B, 2 x A, 1 x B, 3 x A, 1 x B, 4 x A, 1 x B, 3 x A, 1 x B, 2 x A, 1 x B, 1 x A.

11 Repeat on each eye pin – 322 beads in all. Form a ⅛in/2mm loop in the top of each eye pin.

12 For the top band of the pot, cut a 14in/35cm length of wire.

13 Form a ⅛in/2mm loop in one end. Thread the wire through a loop at the top of an eye pin.

14 Onto the top band of wire, thread on the following beads: 2 x A, 1 x C, 2 x A, slide on the next eye pin, repeat until each eye pin is threaded into the top band and the beading pattern is even.

15 Trim the top band wire leaving 1½in/3.75cm excess.

16 Make a loop in the end and hook the loop onto the first loop.

17 To make the scalloped edge, cut seven lengths of wire 3¼in/8cm long.

18 Form a small open loop at one end of each wire.

19 On each thread the following seed beads; 4 x A, 1 x B, 1 x A, 1 x B, 4 x A.

20 Form an open loop at the free end. Bend each wire into a crescent.

21 Loop one open end of a crescent wire onto the top band next to a bead C.

22 Use flat-nosed pliers to bend the loop closed. Pick up the opposite end with pliers and attach it to the wire between the 9th and 10th beads.

23 Close the loop onto the wire. Continue around the top beaded band.

24 Bend the whole form with your fingers, pushing the wire ribbing to form around a small pot or glass bowl.

25 Fill with fresh cut flowers or a small topiary herb plant.

▶ 9 5

embossed velvet tablecloth

This innovative and remarkably simple technique of embossing using store-bought rubber stamps makes a truly stunning cloth. Laden with motifs of fruits and flowers, this cloth could be adapted for any seasonal theme. Polyester velvet can be washed and hung to drip dry, but pressing or ironing will flatten the pile.

MATERIALS

◆ *Rayon or polyester velvet –*
1¼yd/1.25m square, or dimensions to
suit your table
◆ *Selection of large rubber stamps*
4–5in/10–12cm
◆ *Iron*
◆ *Workbench*
◆ *Sewing thread to match the velvet*
◆ *Sewing kit*

1 Select two or three complementary large rubber stamp designs.

2 Decide on the approximate position of each stamp – make a sketch, or mark the back of the velvet with a piece of chalk. Keep the pattern random.

3 Choose one stamp and clamp it to your workbench. This will stop the stamp from moving which can cause double images.

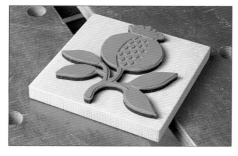

4 Place the velvet over the rubber stamp, nap side down, where you want the image to appear.

5 Take a hot, dry iron and firmly press down onto the back of the velvet over the rubber stamp. Hold for five seconds. Use the heel of the iron, avoiding the steam holes as these will leave an impression.

6 Repeat this process with all the rubber stamps to complete your design.

7 To finish the edge of the tablecloth, roll in the edges of the velvet to the wrong side and blindhem stitch in place.

twig reindeer

These twig reindeer are simple to make using the branches of a dogwood tree.

MATERIALS
◆ *Selection of dry dogwood branches and twigs*
◆ *Prunning shears*
◆ *Hot glue gun and glue*
◆ *Natural color twine*
◆ *Embroidery needle*

1 Cut four pieces of a medium-thick branch 3in/8cm long for each body.

2 For a front leg and the head cut a branched twig 9in/24cm long and 1½in /4cm long where it branches off for the head.

3 For the second front leg, cut one twig 5½in/14cm long matching the thickness to the first leg. Cut this twig at a sharp angle at the top.

4 From a forked branch, cut the antlers 5in/12cm long, with a ½in/1cm stem.

5 Cut the back legs in the same way, ensuring the height matches the front legs, and the form will stand evenly.

6 Using the glue gun, stick together the twigs to form the body. Press the twigs together firmly to form a flat panel.

7 Glue on the head/front leg, attaching it to the front side of the body.

8 Add the second front leg to the other side of the body.

9 Adhere the stem at the top of the back legs to the rear of the body.

10 Glue the antlers to the back of the head.

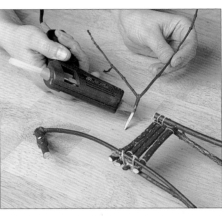

11 Thread an embroidery needle with a length of natural colored twine and wrap the thread around the point where the head and antlers join. Tie the ends to secure, then trim the ends close to the twigs.

12 In the same way wrap twine around the leg and body joints on the front and back of the deer.

chocolate wreath

★

Gigantic chocolate ladybugs, smiling bumble bees and bright butterflies are sure to make this wreath a winner with children.

MATERIALS
◆ *Two squares of heavy-weight corrugated cardboard 22in/55cm*
◆ *Large bundle of pine branches*
◆ *Foil wrapped chocolates – five or six very large and 30 medium or small in assorted designs*
◆ *Hot glue gun and glue*
◆ *Florists' wire*
◆ *Plastic drinking straw*
◆ *Scissors*
◆ *Craft knife and cutting mat*
◆ *Skewer or leather hole punch*
◆ *Pin and string*

1 Draw a 50cm/20in diameter circle on one piece of corrugated cardboard. Tie a pencil to a length of string. Measure 10in/25cm along the string and tie the other end to the pin. Stick the pin in the center of the board.

Hold the pencil taut and draw a circle. Center a second circle inside the first, 8in /20cm diameter. Cut out the circles. Discard the center and the outer edges.

2 Place the wreath on the second piece of cardboard eiththe corrugated lines in opposite directions. Adhere the cut shape to the uncut board using a hot glue gun. Allow to dry. Cut the second piece of cardboard.

3 Using the point of a skewer, make two holes 3in/7.5cm from the edge of the cardboard wreath and 3in/7.5cm apart.

4 Push one straw through each hole until the end is flush with the surface at the back of the board. Glue in place and allow to dry. The straws prevent the hanging wires from tearing the cardboard.

5 Cut one 10in/25cm length of wire and thread through both holes, twist the ends together at the back of the wreath to form a hanging wire.

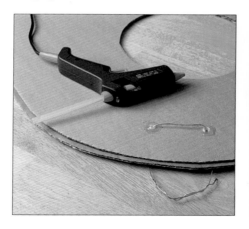

6 Arrange the largest chocolates in an even pattern on the front of the wreath. Glue the foil in place.

7 Cut long twigs of pine to cover the inside edge of the wreath. Cut shorter twigs to fit between the chocolates. Add twigs to the outside, radiating out from the center. Keep the edges neat and even. Cover any bare areas so that the cardboard cannot be seen.

8 Glue the remainder of the chocolates onto the pine.

a c o r n   a n d   v i n e   w r e a t h

★

Carefully prune honeysuckle vines and weave them together into a wreath while they are still pliable.

MATERIALS

◆ *Long lengths of honeysuckle vine*
◆ *24 acorns*
◆ *48 oak leaves*
◆ *Gold spray paint*
◆ *Florists' wire*
◆ *Flat-nose pliers*
◆ *0.6mm brass wire*

1 Cut long lengths of fresh green vine, leaving on all sides shoots and twigs. Make the longest length into a hoop. Twist lengths together using florists' wire to make the desired size hoop.

2 Work around the base hoop, adding in branches by twisting in their ends with florists' wire.

3 Working on a newspaper covered surface, spray clean, dry oak leaves with gold paint. Allow to dry.

4 Cut the brass wire into 6in/15cm lengths and wrap around the stems of the gold leaves. Leave a wire stem to attach to the wreath.

5 Cut 5in/12cm lengths of florists' wire. Push each end of each wire into two

acorns using pliers. As the nut dries it will shrink around the wire.

6 Wrap the acorn wires around the wreath, then add the oak leaves.

mistletoe kissing bough

Galvanized steel wire forms the sturdy base for this delicate mistletoe kissing wreath.

MATERIALS
◆ *1lb/0.5kg of ⅛in/2mm galvanized steel wire*
◆ *1lb/0.5kg of 0.9mm galvanized steel wire*
◆ *Very fine florists' or beading wire*

◆ *24 small silver bells*
◆ *Round-nose pliers*
◆ *Flat-nose pliers*
◆ *Wire cutters*
◆ *Pencil*
◆ *Large bunch of mistletoe*

1 From ⅛in/2mm wire cut one length 43in/110cm and one length 67in/170cm for the top and bottom loops.

2 Using round-nose pliers, and beginning at one end, form four loops in the longer length of wire, each 15in/38cm apart. Twist the opposite end around to form a wreath and thread through the first loop.

3 Repeat with the second length of wire, this time making the loops 11½in/29cm apart.

4 From 0.9mm wire, cut eight lengths 1¾yd/160cm long. Cut twelve lengths 35in/90cm.

5 Make eight springs using four of each 0.9mm lengths of wire. To form a spring, wrap the length of wire tightly around a pencil. Slide the coil from the pencil and open out the last loop from the coil at each end.

6 Attach the four shorter springs to the loops in the small wire wreath. The springs hang below the wreath.

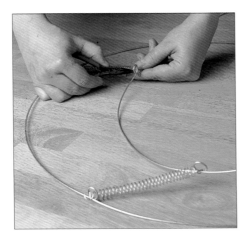

7 Attach the opposite end of each spring to a loop in the larger wire wreath.

8 Attach the four long springs to the loops in the small wire wreath to hang above the wreath. Twist the opposite ends of the four loops together with a scrap of wire.

9 To make the four wire bows, using two 35in/90cm lengths of wire, form a bow

leaving 12in/30cm tails. Twist in a loop at the knot point. Wrap the tails tightly around a pencil to form a spring. Pull the springs into the desired position.

10 Attach one silver bell to the end of each spring.

11 Using the remaining four lengths of wire, make one large bow for the top for the wreath. Add bells as before.

12 Cut a 4in/10cm length of 0.9mm wire. Thread the wire through the large bow and the four springs at the top of the small wreath. Twist the ends together.

13 To make the hanging wire, from 0.9mm wire cut one length 24in/60cm. Form a spring with half of it, then bend the other half into a hook. Attach the spring to the top of the large bow and use the hook to hang the wreath up.

14 To make four jump rings, from 0.9mm wire cut one length 4in/10cm. Wrap tightly around a pencil. Remove the pencil. Using wire cutters, snip the spring, cut-

ting complete single circles of wire. Use these jump rings to attach the small bows to the bottom loops in the larger wreath. Bend the two ends shut.

15 Cut twigs of mistletoe into 5in/13cm forked lengths. Use fine wire to attach the mistletoe in layers to the two wreaths. Wrap securely as mistletoe shrinks as it dries.

▶ 101

PUTTING IT TOGETHER

pine cone gatepost decoration

For a seasonal welcome to your home, make these grand scale artificial pine cones.

MATERIALS

- ◆ 20in/50cm diameter florists' dry foam ball
- ◆ 25in/64cm diameter florists' dry foam ball
- ◆ Large pack of 0.6mm florists' wire 8in/20cm long

- ◆ 100 small and medium pine cones
- ◆ One very large pine cone
- ◆ 24 artificial berries on wire stems
- ◆ 24 pecans in shells
- ◆ 24 short pine sprays
- ◆ Twelve pine twigs 4in/10cm long
- ◆ Flat-nose pliers
- ◆ Wire cutters
- ◆ A length of ½in/1.25mm florists' wire 36in/90cm long

- ◆ One screw 1½in/4cm
- ◆ Screwdriver
- ◆ Drill
- ◆ 4in/10cm square of plywood ¾in/2cm thick
- ◆ 7in/18cm square of plywood ¾in/2cm thick
- ◆ Green spray paint

1 To make a base, center the smaller plywood square on the larger square. Drill three holes across the center, 1in/2.5cm apart, through both pieces of wood. Screw the two pieces together through the central hole.

2 Spray paint the base green.

3 Cut the large foam ball in half. Discard one section.

4 Place the small ball on the flat cut section of the large ball. Thread half of the 36in/90cm length of wire through the center of

the small ball, then through the half ball. Bend the free end of the wire and thread it down through both forms in the same way.

5 Thread the wire ends though the two remaining holes in the base. Twist the ends together under the base and flatten out against the plywood.

6 Wrap florists' wire tightly around the base of each pinecone, leaving a 6in/15cm stem.

7 Beginning at the bottom of the form, insert the wire of the small pinecones in place.

Work around the form. Increase the size of the cones as you work up the form, then decrease the size at the top. Leave a 3in/7.5cm surface bare at the top of the form. Press the pine cones close together so that they grip each other.

8 Use the berries to fill in any small gaps. To attach wires to pecans, using a pair of wire cutters, snip off one pointed end of the shell and thread a wire through. Use these for larger gaps.

9 Wrap wire around tufts of pine and push them in between the pine cones.

10 To finish, arrange the pine twigs across the top of the bare form with needles showing. Secure each in place with a wire bent into a hairpin shape.

11 Wrap the base of the large top pine cone with two or three wires and press into the foam through the pine twigs.

12 Attach to the gatepost with heavy duty twine or garden wire. Hide the base with foliage.

▶ 103

templates

frosted window stencil

Enlarge to fit your window pane

Enlarge to fit your window pane

frosted window stencil
Enlarge to fit your window pane

swiss paper-cut
Enlarge the design
to fit your window

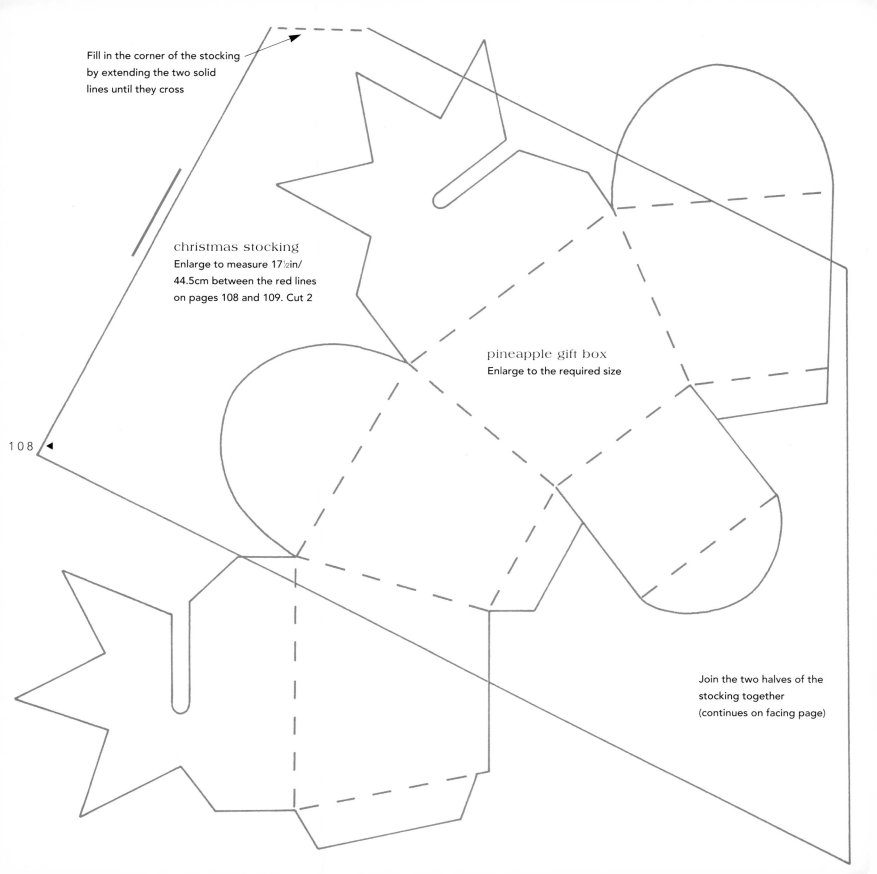

Fill in the corner of the stocking by extending the two solid lines until they cross

christmas stocking
Enlarge to measure 17½in/ 44.5cm between the red lines on pages 108 and 109. Cut 2

pineapple gift box
Enlarge to the required size

108 ◄

Join the two halves of the stocking together (continues on facing page)

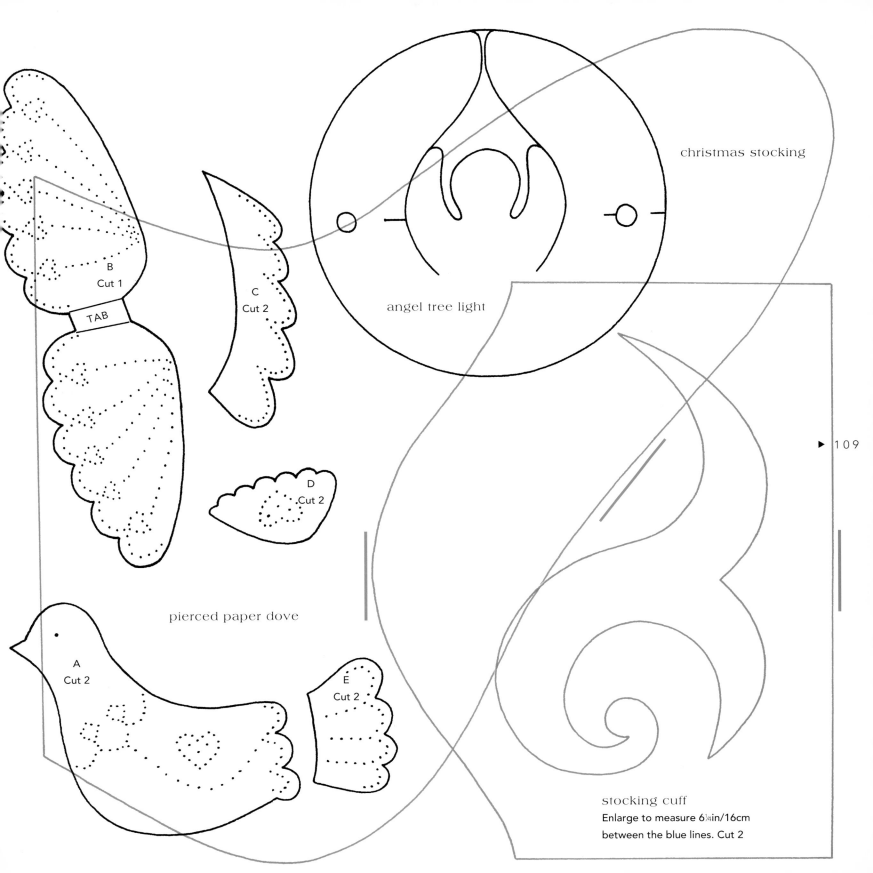

christmas stocking

angel tree light

B
Cut 1

TAB

C
Cut 2

D
Cut 2

pierced paper dove

A
Cut 2

E
Cut 2

► 109

stocking cuff
Enlarge to measure 6¼in/16cm
between the blue lines. Cut 2

cut-paper shelf edging
Half of the image is shown. Reverse the
image on the broken line on the left.
Increase the depth between the blue lines
to 5¼in/13cm

felt tree skirt
Holly leaf 1

felt tree skirt
Holly leaf 2

herald angel
Enlarge to measure 14½in/36.75cm
between the red lines

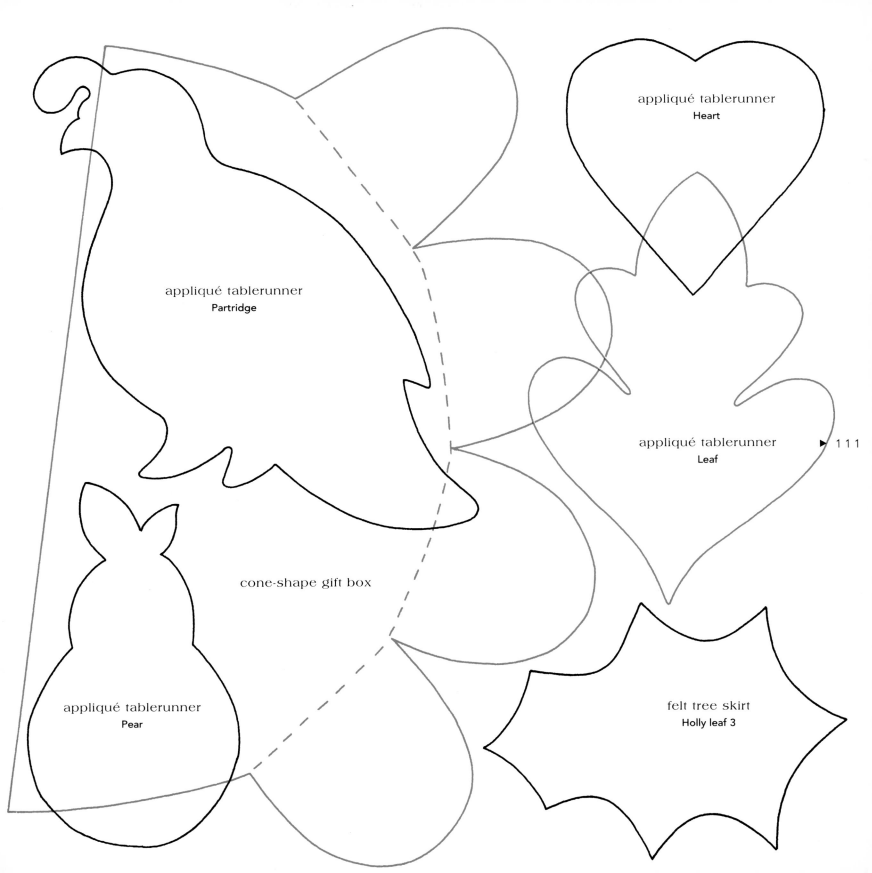

appliqué tablerunner
Heart

appliqué tablerunner
Partridge

appliqué tablerunner
Leaf

▶ 111

cone-shape gift box

appliqué tablerunner
Pear

felt tree skirt
Holly leaf 3

index

112 ◀